Magnify Your Business

Tips, Tools and Strategies for Growing Your Business or Your Nonprofit

MARIA SEMPLE

authorHOUSE

AuthorHouse™
1663 Liberty Drive
Bloomington, IN 47403
www.authorhouse.com
Phone: 1 (800) 839-8640

© 2015 Maria Semple. All rights reserved.

No part of this book may be reproduced, stored in a retrieval system, or transmitted by any means without the written permission of the author.

Published by AuthorHouse   10/20/2015

ISBN: 978-1-5049-5374-0 (sc)
ISBN: 978-1-5049-5373-3 (e)

Print information available on the last page.

Any people depicted in stock imagery provided by Thinkstock are models, and such images are being used for illustrative purposes only. Certain stock imagery © Thinkstock.

This book is printed on acid-free paper.

Because of the dynamic nature of the Internet, any web addresses or links contained in this book may have changed since publication and may no longer be valid. The views expressed in this work are solely those of the author and do not necessarily reflect the views of the publisher, and the publisher hereby disclaims any responsibility for them.

This book is dedicated to my father-in-law, Robert F. Semple. He had the courage to take me under his wing and showed me what it meant to run a business with integrity, all while gaining utmost respect and devotion from his clients.

Contents

Book Reviews ix
Disclaimer xiii
Foreword xv
Introduction xvii

Chapter One: What's Your USP? 1
Chapter Two: Who Are Your Ideal Clients? 17
Chapter Three:
    What's Your First Online Presence? 33
Chapter Four: In-Person Networking 55
Chapter Five:
    Harnessing the Power of Email Marketing 71
Chapter Six:
    Prospecting Strategies to Build Your List 81
Chapter Seven: If only I Had an App
    for That…Resources to Get
    the Most Out of Your Time 91
Chapter Eight:
    Feeding and Maintaining Your Tribe 99

Final Thoughts… 107
Acknowledgements 113

Book Reviews

"*Magnify Your Business*" is one of the smartest business books I've read recently. It's filled with practical wisdom, simple and efficient tools, and specific strategies to help you grow your business to the next level, and then the level beyond that. Maria is a master of showing us how to find opportunities both online and locally and how to make the most of them.

-Sue Urda,
Co-Founder of Powerful You! Women's Network

Maria Semple gives no-nonsense, practical advice in *Magnify Your Business*, which makes it a gem to read and use as an ongoing reference as your business grows. Not only does she give step-by-step ideas about designing your marketing plan, but she also provides great insight into online tools you can use to make the process easier. The good news is that she doesn't forget powerful traditional marketing techniques, like networking, to round out the myriad ways you can grow your business and connect with your tribe.

-Karyn Greenstreet
Small Business Coach/Consultant
and Mastermind Group Expert

"Need to find the right people to talk to and smartly engage them? Your help is here!"

-Tony Martignetti
Host, Tony Martignetti Nonprofit Radio

In *Magnify Your Business*, Maria Semple has managed to put 10 pounds of business advice in a 5 pound book. What also sets her apart is providing her own specific, proven prospect-finding approaches, in addition to sharing a myriad of business and reference resources that are easily accessible. Maria shares both online and offline guidance, which is a critical strategy for all business owners and non-profits who want to become a known entity in their respective industries. I look forward to adding this book to my own reference library as well as recommending it to my clients and colleagues!

-Christine Clifton,
The Business Conversation Expert,
Mindful Business Matters

"This is a must read book for all small business owners and nonprofit executives. Maria pulls together all of her expertise in a clear, concise format. Nonprofits and small business owners alike will find great tips in this book which will propel them to the next level. "Magnify Your Business" is a great read for growing your company online and in your community.

-Dennis C. Miller
President and CEO of Dennis C. Miller Associates, Inc.

"Maria Semple has really done it - and not a moment too soon for us at Answers Design Group! Her new *Magnify Your Business* is a timely, informative and extremely helpful book about affordable tips and strategies for growing your business. Her book is written in a down-to-earth style that gives small business owners hope of being able to accomplish many of the things she suggests. If you want to take your business up to the next level, you simply can't afford NOT to read her book!"

-Val Waterman
Principal, Answers Design Group

Having done social media trainings with Maria Semple, it's no surprise to me that she would write a book with such practical and useful information and resources. *Magnify Your Business* is a great book for anyone who is starting a company or a nonprofit.

-Geri Stengel
President and Founder
Ventureneer

A quick and easy read, which covers all the basics for anyone starting their own business.

-Amy Eisenstein,
ACFRE
Author, Speaker, Consultant

Disclaimer

Many of the designations used by manufacturers and sellers to distinguish their products are claimed as trademarks. Where those designations appear in this book and the author is aware of a trademark claim, the designations have been indicated.

The Publisher and the Author make no representations or warranties with respect to the accuracy or completeness of the contents of this work and specifically disclaim all warranties, including without limitation warranties of fitness for a particular purpose. No warranty may be created or extended by sales or promotional materials. The advance and strategies contained herein may not be suitable for every situation. This work is sold with the understanding that the Publisher is not engaged in rendering legal, accounting, or other professional services.

If professional assistance is required the services of a competent professional person should be sought. Neither the Publisher nor the Author shall be liable for damages arising herefrom. The fact that an organization or website is referred to in this work as a citation and/or a potential source of further information does not mean that the Author or the Publisher endorses the information the organization or website may provide or recommendations is may make. Further, readers should be aware that internet websites listed in this work may have changed or disappeared between when this work was written and when it is read.

Foreword

So very many times you read business marketing books from "experts" who profess to have the magic solution to all of our business needs. These "experts" just spout out theory and repeat ideas that they read on the internet or in some other expert's business book. They have actually never really been in the unique shoes of you the entrepreneur or not for profit. This book is different. Maria Semple is truly a small business and nonprofit expert. She walks in your shoes every day and has worked closely with so many exactly like you. The concepts she will share are real. They are authentic. They are honest. I have personally have had the pleasure of working with Maria for almost ten years now. Trust me, she knows her stuff! I watch her in action delivering workshops and keynotes across the country and I am just in awe of her. She inspires small business owners and not for profit leaders with her knowledge and expertise and most importantly her willingness to share!

Maria's spirit for navigating us through this crowded space inspires me each and every day! I'm

Maria Semple

so honored to know her personally and have the chance to work closely with her. I know you will find in this book solid tactics on how to connect with new customers and reconnect with old. She will help organize you and give structure.

You have a unique opportunity in this day and age. We are able to do things digitally with technology that we never even thought possible. Yes, it can be completely overwhelming. I promise you that Maria will break it all down for you with straightforward ideas that she just didn't read about. These are tactics she has used successfully for her own business as well as for her many happy clients. So no more excuses. Get a highlighter, note pad and a cup of coffee and let's get down to business! Wishing you the best in business and life!

Wendi Caplan-Carroll-Area Director, Constant Contact

Introduction

This book is for the entrepreneurs among us, those independent spirits who see a need and have a great idea for meeting it. You may have a one-person shop, run a small business with a growing staff, or oversee a not-for-profit organization serving the community in some way. Regardless of the business model you have chosen, you know that you have something valuable to offer. You just need to connect with those who need and support it.

I have great news for you. You have access to media platforms that are faster and more powerful than ever. Entrepreneurs and nonprofits no longer need costly television or print advertising to reach the masses; word-of-mouth is no longer a plodding exercise in self-promotion. On the other hand, the scope and variety of resources can be overwhelming to the newcomer. The wrong choices can, in fact, run up costs without reaching the *right* people: those who would benefit the most from your product or service. It is hard to know where and how to begin. Throughout this book you'll see tips that apply to both for-profit and non-profit entities. Don't let your tax status dictate a separate set of rules for magnifying and growing your venture!

Audiences have changed as well. Today's consumers live in a noisy marketplace. It takes a new approach to capture and to hold their attention. It takes a new set of strategies—you might call it a new version of word-of-mouth—to earn their trust, and their business. The buzzword these days is "engagement," but I like to think of it as a conversation with a purpose. It is a conversation that is mediated by technology, but when done well it can lead to loyal customers and, through their endorsement, market growth.

"Magnify Your Business" will help you to cut through the noise so that you and your audience can find each other. Over the last twenty years I have worked with hundreds of clients whose ultimate marketing goal is the same as yours: to connect, in a productive and lasting way, with potential customers. I helped them design and implement marketing strategies that are as efficient as they are effective, and I can do the same for you.

Let's get started!

* * * * *

Chapter One: What's Your USP?

No, I'm not referring to psychic powers or your cholesterol level.

Your USP is your Unique Selling Proposition. A USP describes your product or service, but it is *not* the product or service description that you've included in your business plan. It is the language you'll use to set your business apart from everyone else who does work similar to you. How do you differ? What unique skills do you bring to the table? What value do you add? Your business plan, on the other hand, is a vital strategic and operational road map designed for an audience of you and perhaps other managers at your organization, as well as potential investors. Although functional and thorough, I doubt that there is much in your business plan that would roll off your tongue without tripping over itself.

The USP speaks to a different audience. It shifts the lens from what interests management and investors to what interests your targeted clients and customers. It is light and portable, traveling from handshake to business card to website-- to convey in an instant what is special about what you do. And let's face it, consumer attention lasts hardly a minute so you need to be quick!

> *"Make an instant impression of how your product or service solves a problem."*

Think about it: Does an auto salesman hand you the "product description" section of Ford Motor Corporation®'s entire strategic business plan when you ask to test drive a car? How about the Xerox® representative, when she visits your office to give a presentation about copiers? Citibank® or Chase® managers, when they seek your business? No, they don't. And if they did, would you as a consumer, really care? As a consumer, your focus is on how each company proposes to help you, whether it is to replace an old car, upgrade a copier, or open a checking account. You don't have time to waste so you want this insight, say, yesterday, right? Successful companies know this, and so they spend considerable resources on making an instant impression of how their product or service is uniquely qualified to solve your particular problem.

If you were to picture a line of communication going from you to every potential client, the USP would be the first half of that line (we'll get to the second half in Chapter Two). Your targeted customers are not interested in your strategic plan; *they are interested in what you can do for them. What problem are you solving differently or better than someone else?* Creating a clear, concise and compelling USP that sets you apart from your competition is the first step in helping your prospective clients understand why your product or service is worth their attention and, hopefully, their business. Your USP is a big part of your Brand Promise. What does your business or nonprofit really stand for? In the words of Simon Sinek, it's discovering your "Why". An example is Tom's® Shoes and their model of "One for One". What originated as a business model of giving one pair of shoes to someone in need for every pair bought, has expanded to include eyewear, water, coffee and bags.

The next time you are at a networking or professional event, pay attention to how people introduce themselves and their businesses. It is likely that, in some way, they are communicating their USP. It is what sets their enterprise apart from the rest. For example, Claudia Mott, founder of the financial advising firm Epona Financial Solutions, focuses her business on women, in particular those who are going through or have gone through divorce. Claudia introduces her USP by saying that she "Helps women answer the question: 'Am I going to be all right?'" She presents her USP in a way that is clear, approachable and—importantly—inspires confidence in her abilities. Even though I do not fit her niche market I would be inclined to refer her to someone who did, partly because I know and trust her, but also because I know exactly who her ideal client is.

It can be challenging to create the right USP. Try to create it as a value proposition, not as a "data dump." Here are a few strategies that can help get you thinking in the right direction:

- Make a list of those who you perceive to be your competitors. See what they are saying about themselves and think about what you can, and want to do differently and better. Is there something special about your background or expertise that could lead to a niche market? What do you bring to the table that is unique?

- If you have already been providing goods or services to customers, why not ask them what they found to be most valuable in their dealings with you? You might be surprised at what you learn. Perhaps they were particularly impressed with your excellent turnaround time, or appreciated your focus on customer service. What sets you apart for current customers may prove to be a selling point for new customers as well.

- Think about your product or service in the form of an "imagine statement." First, envision the people or businesses that you most want to serve. Then, state how you want to solve their problem or fulfill their need.

I have used all of these strategies over time, but found that the imagine statement exercise really helped me to hone in on the essence of what I do best. I am a Master Certified Solution Provider for Constant Contact®. It is a great credential for work that I enjoy, but with hundreds of Master Certified Solution Providers in the U.S., I have a lot of competition. It is critical that I focus on what it is that I do that is different from the rest, so that the people and businesses who would benefit most from my expertise—nonprofit organizations prospecting for new donors and businesses prospecting for new clients—will know that I am uniquely qualified to help them. Here is my imagine statement:

> *Imagine having all of the prospects that your business needs, as well as the roadmap for connecting with those prospects. My name is Maria Semple and my business is The Prospect Finder. I can help you prospect, connect and prosper.*

Imagining how your clients' lives will be made better by your product or service will help you craft communications that resonate with the listeners and readers you most want to reach. This exercise works for community organizations as well. In the nonprofit sector, it is often referred to as a "vision statement," but the idea is the same: to think about what you do from the perspective of those you do it for. Here are a few great examples of nonprofit organization vision statements:

Make-A-Wish®: *Our vision is that people everywhere will share the power of a wish.*

Kiva: *We envision a world where all people—even in the most remote areas of the globe—hold the power to create opportunity for themselves and others.*

Save the Children®: *We envision a world in which every child attains the right to survival, protection, development and participation.*

Creating the right language is the first and most important step in creating your USP, but also consider how it can be expressed in other ways as well. Let's revisit your trip to the car dealership. Think about the language and pictures in brochures and print ads, the music in television ads, and the design of the websites that you viewed as you prepared for your test drive. How about the architectural design of the dealership itself, the dress and manner of the employees, and the availability of snacks and beverages? Don't forget the allure of "new car smell." A complete sensory image has been created for you.

> ***"Create and project a unique personality for your brand."***

Stop in at a dealership for another car manufacturer and you will see just as much attention to the details of your experience, but the details themselves will be different. For example, a luxury brand might require salespeople to wear designer suits, while a more family-oriented brand might prefer that its sales force wear casual clothing. One might offer customers high-end sparkling water while the other offers juice and coffee. With so many brands on the market, each manufacturer must create a unique personality and then project that personality to its ideal customers.

You can adapt these strategies for your business too. I frequent a consignment shop that specializes in "new line recycled" merchandise. They carry only high-end items, and provide the kind of customer attention you would usually expect from a high-end retail store. Every detail, from their Facebook page (which offers coupons to new "fans") to their shopping bags (which are funky and fun to re-use), reflects their ideal clientele and contributes to a particular customer experience.

Don't worry if it takes a few tries to craft a USP that works for you. Once you find the words that feel right you will be surprised at how much easier it is to speak about your business. It will also become much easier to choose the other elements—visual, audio, and physical—that best express your USP.

You should also expect that your USP will evolve over time. Just as your business plan will be updated from time to time, it is important to review your USP now and then to make sure that it continues to provide a clear sense of who you are, what you do that is special and how you stand behind what you do.

Whether you are a business looking for customers or a nonprofit organization reaching out to donors, you are asking people to place their money, and therefore their trust, with you. When it comes to communicating your USP, clarity and confidence go hand in hand. And when you demonstrate confidence in yourself and your work, others will be confident in you as well.

In the next chapter, we will begin developing your prospecting and communications plan. But before we get to nuts and bolts, I would like for you to take a minute to consider your future as an entrepreneur. Why are you considering launching a new business or nonprofit initiative?

Entrepreneurs are, by nature, independent spirits who want to make their own path to success. I am an entrepreneur and I think it is a great way to work and live. If this is your path as well, you are probably already aware that success depends entirely on you. This means that you are responsible for every aspect of your venture, from product or service provision to marketing, accounting, customer service, as well as legal and tax compliance. What it *doesn't* mean is that you have to actually perform all of those tasks.

> *"Decide which tasks should be handled by another professional."*

Take a hard look at all that needs to be done to build a solid foundation for your business or nonprofit, and decide which tasks could, and should, be handled by another professional. For me, that translates into hiring someone to help me keep my expense accounting under control. What takes her two hours to complete would take me four or more—time that I can better utilize by serving current clients or prospecting for new ones. When I compare the cost of the bookkeeper against the cost of lost revenue, it is easy to see that I can't afford *not* to hire one.

This holds true for nonprofit enterprises as well as for-profit businesses. Small organizations often work staff and volunteers into early burnout in the name of saving a few dollars. But when you analyze the cost vs. opportunities lost, can you honestly say that you are providing the best possible service that you can to your community? What, really, is the best way to build a sustainable future for your organization?

Take stock of what your own skill set is like, and remember that it is okay if you don't happen to possess every skill that is needed to run a business. Make a list of the expertise that you need and then search for the best partner you can afford to make that system happen for you. In fact, by the time you finish reading this book, you may decide it is in your best interest to hire someone to handle some or all of your online marketing. If so, you will be a knowledgeable client. And you will be helping another entrepreneur build his or her business.

"Plan your work and work your plan." That's one of the first things my father-in-law, businessman and consultant Robert F. Semple, taught me when I set out to build my own business, The Prospect Finder LLC.

If you are reading this book, chances are good (or at least I hope they are) that you have already put time and effort into developing a business plan. You have analyzed your market and your competition, and have thought through how your business will operate and how it will be financed until it can finance itself.

If you are launching a new community initiative, you should fully explore how the need you have identified might be met through collaboration with a more established organization before launching a new nonprofit corporation. According to the Urban Institute's National Center on Charitable Statistics, in 2012 73% of charitable organizations' revenue came from program service revenues (including government contracts). Another 6% came from dues, memberships, and product sales. Only 21% came from private donations and government grants[1]. I strongly caution you to think long and hard before launching an organization that relies on donations to meet more than 20% of its budget.

If you have not yet created your business plan, I recommend that you take the time to do so. There are a variety of government agencies and private organizations that are devoted to helping entrepreneurs build businesses out of great ideas. Here are a few to get you started:

SBA.gov
The U.S. Small Business Administration offers a wealth of information about planning and starting a new business venture.

- Local offices throughout the country provide counseling, information about loan opportunities, and more: https://www.sba.gov/tools/local-assistance/districtoffices

- The national website also offers a page devoted to business plans: https://www.sba.gov/writing-business-plan

- Information about choosing your business structure (a decision that will have legal and tax implications), can be found at: https://www.sba.gov/category/navigation-structure/starting-managing-business/starting-business/choose-your-business-stru

- A list of local Small Business Development Centers can be found here: https://www.sba.gov/tools/local-assistance/sbdc

Entrepreneur.com
This site offers a step-by-step guide to developing a business plan: http://www.entrepreneur.com/businessplan/index.html

bPlans
bPlans provides guidance and free sample business plans to follow: http://www.bplans.com/

Grantspace.com
This site's "Knowledge Base" provides a curated list of resources for those who want to develop a business plan for a nonprofit organization: http://grantspace.org/tools/knowledge-base/Nonprofit-Management/Establishment/business-plans

SCORE
This organization offers free person-to-person mentoring for entrepreneurs as well as online information. You can learn more at www.score.org.

> In addition to these resources, check out what's being offered by your local community college or high school-based adult education program, and by your local public library as well.

* * * * *

Chapter Two: Who Are Your Ideal Clients?

In Chapter One, we focused on your unique selling proposition, or who *you*, as a business, are. Your USP message is the first half of the line connecting you to your client base. Now let's take a look at the second half: Who *they* are.

In this chapter we will focus on developing your initial concept of your target market into a deeper understanding of the people you most want to reach and engage. Who are your ideal clients? What is important to them? What are their concerns? Where will they look first when they are trying to find a solution to the problem that you are prepared to solve? *Wherever that is, that's where you want to be with your USP message.*

Here are the questions that you want to ask, now and regularly in the future, to ensure that your business becomes, and remains, relevant and valued to your target market:

- Who are my ideal clients?
- Where are they?

- What is important to them?
- How do they perceive the problem that I aim to solve?
- Where are they likely to look for solutions to this problem?

Let's take a closer look at each of these questions.

Who are my ideal clients?

One great concept can lead to multiple client channels. Which channel will be yours? When I was doing research for this book, I learned that in large cities it is possible to access dry cleaning services online. Consumers can "book" door-to-door dry cleaning services from a website, with a few clicks of a mouse. What a great idea for busy professionals with the resources to pay a premium for an everyday service! It is also an idea that presents a variety of potential ideal markets. You might choose to target attorneys who work long days, and so focus your business on very early morning or late night pick-up and delivery times. Or perhaps you are targeting wealthy families with children. In this case, you might focus on hours that coincide with childcare staff schedules. One enterprising dry cleaner dominated his local market by having one centralized plant and setting up satellite locations for customers to drop off their cleaning. Vans delivered the finished product to each neighborhood drop-off location. Another cleaner met commuters at the train platform to collect their clothing, then returned the cleaned items there the next day. Then again, maybe your target is not the dry cleaning customer at all. Your USP might be to provide software design and support for this service, and so your ideal clients may be the dry cleaners in upscale urban areas. If that is the case, you will want to be thinking about the needs of the owners of these businesses. What problem or problems will you solve for them?

Where are my ideal clients?

Where do your ideal clients operate? Are you targeting a geographic region? Or can your market space be occupied virtually? It is likely that you have some interesting choices available to you. A writer/editor may choose to focus on a particular geographic area, because her USP includes a focus on face-to-face interaction with clients. The ability to visit her clients at their place of business is an important factor in the services she provides. Another writing/editing business might have a completely different approach, providing quick, accurate results via the Internet, and with minimal client interaction. For example, Michele Hickey of Silver Lining Communications is a writer serving those lacking the time to generate their own proposals and completed manuscripts, serving them wherever they are, virtually.

What is important to them?

Successful entrepreneurs are thinking about their clients all the time. In fact, they are usually thinking about what it is that their clients might be thinking about. They continually question and test their assumptions about their target market, staying the course but also staying flexible. It's easy to do this when you are meeting new people at networking events and engaging with people through your blog, social media and e-news. If you are continually sharing great tips and become a trusted resource, you'll easily get feedback about whatever you're sharing. The beauty of entrepreneurship is the ease with which you can recalibrate your approach to better serve your clients, or to take advantage of a newly identified opportunity.

Some say that the things to which you give your focus expand. If you've ever purchased a new car, you'll know what I mean: suddenly, it seems that you notice that particular make and model around every corner. The same will be true for your new venture. Once you start to live and breathe it, you will be surprised at how many ideas and opportunities show up in unexpected ways. The key here is to stay open-minded and recognize when opportunity knocks. Here's a quick example of what I mean: For a number of years, my business focused solely on serving the nonprofit sector by providing prospect research services profiling high net worth individuals who are major gift prospects. One day I received a call from a financial services firm asking if I could train their financial advisors on how to prospect this lucrative market. It dawned on me that both clients were in need of the same services, but for different reasons.

> *"Use technology to find out what your customers are thinking about."*

Here is one idea to get you started: Let technology help you to keep up with what your customers are thinking about. Use tailored newsfeeds, such as LinkedIn's Pulse or RSS feeds of your favorite bloggers to stay current on topics related to your business and of interest to your ideal clients. Keyword alerts, from services such as Google Alerts, Talkwalker.com or Mention.net, will let you know when a topic you are following is mentioned on the Internet. For example, one of my alerts is set to let me know when the phrase "high net worth" comes up. You can also use alerts to let you know when your company name comes up, or to learn more about a particular prospective client.

How do they perceive the problem that I aim to solve?

One of the best ways to find out what people think is to ask them. Technology makes this easier than ever, with tools like Constant Contact's Survey Tool or Survey Monkey®. Like online newsfeeds and alerts, the learning curve is small and most offer at least some of their services for free. Armed with a ten-question survey and an email list, you can learn what your community thinks about the problem your business addresses. You can even use the process of the survey to grow your list by asking people to pass the survey along to others.

If you feel like you want or need a more in-depth exchange of ideas, you can plan focus groups and informational interviews with selected individuals. In the past that might have meant renting space and compensating participants for their travel expenses, but today much can be accomplished via the Internet, at a much lower price point. Traditionally, Focus Groups are conducted in an interactive group setting, allowing conversations and opinions to be shared. The research is considered qualitative since participants are sharing their beliefs, attitudes and opinions.

If you don't have the budget for conducting formal focus groups, consider using some free or low-cost methods to research your target market. Tools range from free conference lines to tools to do virtual face-to-face meetings. The online meeting tools can even be used from a mobile device. Here are a few of my favorites:

- **FreeConferencePro** enables you to host up to 200 people on a free conference call and you can even record the call so you can share the recording afterward. This is also a great solution to record free Podcasts! Learn more at http://www.freeconferencepro.com. Use this when all you need is a free conference call line. There are no screen-sharing capabilities with this service.

- **GoToMeeting (a Citrix® solution)** has a free version that allows up to three people to participate in an online meeting, but tier pricing is available if you need to increase the number of attendees. With this service, you can enable webcams as well as screen sharing, which is a valuable tool for long-distance meetings and collaboration. Meetings can be recorded as well. Learn more by visiting http://www.gotomeeting.com. This service is best for group meetings and delivering webinars. It serves you best when you need to share visual elements with the other participants.

- **Skype**™ is a free service that can be used for online face-to-face meetings. All users must open a free Skype account. Learn about Skype at http://www.skype.com/en/. Use Skype to meet 'face to face' with someone anywhere in the world. This will be useful if you are trying to gather data or simply get to know someone before entering into a business relationship.

- **Google Hangouts** is another free service for free face-to-face online meetings. All users must open a free Google account. Your hangouts can be public or private and even recorded for future sharing through Hangouts On Air and uploaded to a YouTube account. Learn more at https://plus.google.com/hangouts. In some cases, you might find that the group who wants to meet is already a user of Google services, and there won't be a need to open a separate Skype account for your meetings. Plus, if you choose to do the Hangouts On Air, you'll accumulate additional content that can be used in marketing your business.

Unsure about how to organize and conduct a focus group? Colleges and universities are generous with resources, and the following institutions offer guidebooks and tips specifically related to focus groups—just type "focus group guide" in the search box on each main page listed below:

- Rowan University - www.rowan.edu
- Duke University – www.duke.edu
- Central Connecticut State University – www.ccsu.edu
- Lehigh Universty - http://www1.lehigh.edu
- Eastern Illinois University – www.eiu.edu

Your local community college may offer resources as well. It can't hurt to reach out to the marketing and communications faculty to see if they are looking for hands-on experience for students.

And, let's not forget our helpful local Reference Librarians. They can help you navigate online tools such as ReferenceUSA to research both businesses in your target area as well as the consumers the business will aim to serve. These are fee-based databases that are available for FREE if you use them at your library. I highly recommend discussing your research needs with a librarian to see how they can help you navigate the myriad of resources available to you.

There are more do-it-yourself tools for entrepreneurs than ever, and their availability and variety are astounding. Still, for reasons discussed in Chapter One, you may want to consider hiring a consultant specializing in market research to help you gather and analyze data about your particular customer base. This may be a worthwhile investment, particularly if you are launching a product or service that does not currently exist in your chosen market space. Ultimately, it may save you money by helping you refine your plans based on the feedback gained from the research. This is especially true for new product launches, as it can impact research, development and design costs, as well as marketing expenses.

Where are my ideal clients likely to look for solutions to the problem that my business can solve?

While you are reviewing newsfeeds, tracking alerts and posing survey questions, be sure to gather information about where your ideal clients are looking when they need a problem solver. Google remains the most popular search engine, and is often the first place people go to search for a solution. Try typing in various search terms related to the problem that your business solves and see what comes up. Performing this exercise will be a precursor to finding the key words that should be used on your website and for Search Engine Optimization (SEO). If you have an idea of what your keyword should be, type it into Google – scroll to the bottom and you'll see Google's "related search". This provides you with variations on that term; you can see other search queries that viewers may have used to find a similar topic.

LinkedIn is another important go-to source for many professionals; try searching in that space as well to see what kind of results you get. You can use the search box at the top of the page, or launch into Advanced Search, for more targeted searches. (Much more will be covered on LinkedIn in Chapter 6.)

Continue drilling down to your niche area by seeing what services are promoted, and what promotional opportunities are available through professional associations and publications that appeal to specific markets. For example, nonprofit professionals often look to the Association of Fundraising Professionals, which is a national organization with state-focused chapters. Media outlets targeted to the sector include *The Nonprofit Times*, *The Chronicle of Philanthropy*, and CharityChannel.com.

Another strategy is to keep an eye on your "benchmark" products and services—that list of competitors you examined when you were developing your USP. How are they communicating with their targeted audiences? You can set alerts for your competitors' names to see when and where they are promoting themselves.

Finding Your Tribe

Seth Godin, TED Talk speaker, entrepreneur and author of *Tribes: We Need You to Lead Us*, is quoted as saying that tribes are about "Leading and connecting people and ideas." [1] My advice to you is to find and connect with your own tribe, invited and cultivated to support your business. These are individuals who can offer qualified perspective, insight and support, and who are willing to be honest with you—even when it might hurt a little. And they care enough about you and what you are trying to do to reach out and contribute thoughtfully so that you are not pursuing your goals with blinders on.

> *"Don't work in isolation; seek out advice and counsel from peer advisors."*

Make sure you are connecting with and adding to your tribe on a regular basis. Mastermind groups and peer advisory groups are a popular concept in entrepreneurial circles. I have in the past participated in a local mastermind group that met according to a schedule. Meetings were structured so that everyone in the room had a chance to present his or her current issues and concerns, and to gather feedback from the rest of the group. The experience was extremely

---

[1] Seth Godin's TED Talk, February 2009, Long Beach, CA.

valuable. The regular meetings kept me focused on my overall goals, while the interaction helped me to think outside the box.

The Alternative Board is a virtual mastermind space. Although participation is available for a fee, their website, www.thealternativeboard.com, offers a wealth of free resources including white papers, tips, and survey results. Another site, www.thesuccessalliance.com, will help you to locate an existing peer advisory group. They also provide step-by-step instructions for forming your own. Although I no longer meet regularly with my mastermind group, I keep in touch with them all and am confident that I can reach out to them when I have a business issue and need advice that I can trust. Sometimes, it is important just to be able to talk through a problem with someone who is familiar with your work and who cares enough to contribute his or her insight and experience.

Don't be afraid to include in your tribe other professionals in your field. For example, if you are considering becoming a grant writer for nonprofit organizations, why not develop relationships with other independent grant writers? This strategy might not work with everyone you meet—some might see you as the competition. But more often than not, they will be just as happy to add you to *their* tribe. You may even find yourself collaborating with that person on a future project—especially if either of you has special expertise the other needs.

Don't underestimate the power of referrals, either. A free-lance grant writer that I know appreciates being able to refer professionals to potential clients that she is unable to take on, or that do not fit her particular USP. Although she doesn't get the business, she does build goodwill in her community. On occasion, this type of networking has also landed her work as a subcontractor for larger grant writing and consulting firms.

Hiring yourself out as a subcontractor, by the way, can be a great way to test the waters of a new venture, particularly if you are transitioning out of another full-time career. There is no substitute for hands-on experience to help you understand the realities of the field you are pursuing, while also building your reputation and portfolio.

> *"Engage with other types of professionals operating in your target space."*

Be sure to engage with other types of professionals operating in your target space, too. The grant writer includes in her tribe individuals with experience in marketing, printing and design, social media and education. A variety of perspectives helps her to develop a better understanding of the need for her unique services.

Your venture may require additional schooling or some sort of licensing or certification, and surely you will need to build a corps of professionals in the legal, accounting and insurance fields. Every individual you meet in these areas is a potential member of your tribe as well. Always be on the outlook for good people who bring knowledge and integrity into your circle.

Chapter Three: What's Your First Online Presence?

This is where we begin activating that line between you and your ideal client. If you are reading this book, you are probably already thinking that your business needs some kind of online presence. And you are right. There are several really good reasons for this. First, having an online presence helps to build brand awareness. Think about how often you turn to Google or Bing when you are looking for a new product or service—and then consider how many other people do the very same thing. It is in your best interest to be where the searchers are. In fact, it is imperative in today's world. Otherwise, you risk being nearly invisible. Let's examine some of the components that make up a robust online presence.

Take One, Social Media...

The right online presence can also help to promote customer engagement. Social media is just that: social. Opportunities for dialogue are built into the platforms. You can communicate with your customers, and they can communicate right back. For relatively little effort on your part, you gain an ongoing glimpse into what they are thinking, what they like or don't like and what they need from a business or professional like you.

Finally, an online presence can serve as your digital brochure. But this is no ordinary brochure: it can be updated quickly and easily to adapt to your growing business, it can capture data about those who view it, and it can capture actual, ongoing audience members. All without the cost of printing (and storing!) hundreds of four-color brochures that are likely to be out of date by the time the ink dries. In fact, one of the primary benefits of maintaining social media platforms is its ease to update and real-time capture of conversations with your customers. And, all of this can be done from a smartphone!

The problem, of course, is finding the right starting point. My advice is to start with the basics, focusing on three aspects of the online environment: *location services, social media* and *domain presence*.

Location Services
Location services are especially important if your business relies on bringing customers to where you operate, such as a shop or office. But don't overlook the value of being "found" online, even if you bring

your product or service to your customers' doors. The biggest player on this field is Google My Business (google.com/business/).

Google My Business is free and it takes minimal clicks to add your business address to their system, which includes Google Maps and Google Search. The service captures reviews and provides analytics so you can learn something about those who are locating you online. It is mobile-friendly and, best of all, can be managed from a single dashboard. There are instructions for managing multiple locations too, which may be important as your business grows. It is an excellent starting point for connecting a new business directly to potential customers.

Social Media

Don't be overwhelmed by the social media landscape. Yes, it is growing and changing all the time. And no, you don't want to get sucked into a vortex of relentless updates and profile management. Be selective, especially at the start. Once you develop a rapport with your ideal customers via social media, you will learn which platforms they are using the most, and you can adjust as you go along. In the beginning, though, you will want to establish yourself in a few key arenas.

With more than a *billion* users worldwide, Facebook is still the biggest fish in the social media pond. Therefore, it may be a good social media platform for you. If your company is a B to C, meaning you do business directly with the end consumer (as opposed to doing business with another business), then Facebook is the social media platform preferred by the B to C space. The company provides help and step-by-step instructions at https://www.facebook.com/business/overview. Remember that social media is as much about visual elements as it is about text, so be sure to have a healthy portfolio of logos and photographs to brighten your page. We live in a world with ever shortening attention spans, which means less time spent reading online. Facebook allows you to upload videos, and you can post updates and announcements from other professionals and businesses that relate to your own. It can also be a vehicle for sharing published articles that you think your clients and followers might find interesting or helpful.

It didn't take too much effort on your part to give your business entry into the World Wide Web, did it? And so far it hasn't cost you a dime, either. I'm hoping that by this time you are encouraged to add one or two more social media platforms to your marketing strategy. There are many to choose from and most offer at least a baseline of services that are offered free of charge. But, which ones?

> *"Go where your buyers are, but where your competitors aren't."*

Once again, look to your competition for ideas. Which platforms are they using? How many followers do they have? How do they present their services or products? What do they post? When and how often do they post? What seems to get the strongest response from their community? Understanding which platforms are already dominated by the large competitors might be an opportunity for you to build upon a different platform. In other words, go where your buyers are but not necessarily where your competitors are already entrenched. Go where your competition *isn't*.

Learn the Rules

Every social media platform has a unique personality, and so you will want to choose those that match your USP, and then match your activity to the platform's tone and style. Twitter followers are waiting for the next flurry of activity, while the professionals who use LinkedIn don't necessarily like it when one individual dominates their newsfeed.

They have rules too. For example, personal Facebook accounts may not be used for business purposes, but you need a personal account in order to establish a business page. Learn and follow the rules, and also test your content and timing to learn what resonates with your audience.

Constant Contact offers useful recommendations regarding the most-used social media platforms. Their research covers tone, tolerated frequency of activity, audience, timing, and the best uses for each platform. Ryan Pinkham, Content Manager with Constant Contact, wrote a blog post entitled "How to Create a Social Media Posting Schedule" (Http://blogs.constantcontact.com/social-media-posting-schedule/). In it he offers helpful guidelines for minimum and maximum posting frequencies. For example, as a general rule of thumb, your LinkedIn connections may not want to see more than five postings per week from you. However, Twitter is entirely different. On that platform, the minimum suggested is five Tweets per week, and there is no suggested maximum. Understanding these general guidelines will help you maintain a more engaged following. Once you have decided which platforms are right for your business, you can create a schedule that helps to guide you in creating appropriate messages, and that will help you to manage timely posts.

Pay-to-play is the latest trend in social media, as companies work to monetize their platforms. While it is difficult to say where this trend will lead, and how much it will cost, right now there are entry-level price points that are well worth the expense. For example, Facebook has altered its algorithms so that posts on business pages are not necessarily forwarded to all of your followers' newsfeeds (limiting what the company calls your "organic" reach). You can, however, "boost" important posts for a fee that begins in the $10 range.

A Facebook boost allows you to reach beyond your company's followers, according to a set of parameters that you select. This can include geographic reach, age range and even interests that you define by key words. It is a simple but effective strategy for promoting a special sale or an event, such as a conference or performance.

Since your boosted message will reach new sets of eyes, consider doing it in a way that invites some sort of "opt-in" feature. Perhaps you can offer a coupon or a free download as an incentive? Everyone loves freebies! This is a great opportunity to add followers and to build your mailing list. And as you might guess, the service includes analytics that help you learn more about your audience.

LinkedIn: The Business Toolkit

For those of you who decide to use LinkedIn, know that this company has some interesting features that can be used as powerful prospecting tools. For example, you can send a message to all of your 1st degree LinkedIn connections to ask them to follow your company page. The LinkedIn database can be mined through advanced key word searches that pull on all of your 2nd degree connections and beyond. An auto-delivery option lets you get new results on a scheduled basis so that you proactively prospect for new connections in your target market. No other social media platform currently allows you to put your prospecting on auto-pilot! Who wouldn't want a steady stream of prospects delivered to their doorstep?

In addition to sharing an Update, LinkedIn also allows you to "Publish a Post". These are akin to blog posts and might be a great way for to you to test the waters on blogging. These Published Posts also become part of your LinkedIn profile, resulting in a collection of writings visible on your public profile. Back-end analytics let you see what kind of response your posts are garnering in terms of Comments, Shares and Likes. Your long-form post is also searchable both on and off LinkedIn.

Joining LinkedIn groups that pertain to your business and your clients can be useful as well. This is a great way to share ideas with and learn from your peers, and to have thoughtful conversations with clients, prospects and allied professionals. While idea sharing is welcomed in LinkedIn groups, overtly promotional posts are not. If you are unsure about a post you are planning, contact the group manager first. Another great way to build community is to start your own LinkedIn Group. You can set this to be an Open Group or a Members-Only Group. Deciding on which setting to use really depends on your goals for the Group. A provocative group discussion draws attention to you and your business, sets you up as a thought leader and may result in people eventually seeking out your services. As a business owner or nonprofit organization, if you want to use Groups to grow your online footprint, I highly recommend an Open Group. Closely monitor for spammers, however, since you may find that some people may look to dominate the Group postings with inappropriate or only 'sales-y' content.

Nonprofits often overlook this platform for engaging with potential employers, donors, and volunteers. Don't make this mistake! LinkedIn has set aside a whole department of employees dedicated to your sector. There are services you'll get for free or reduced rates, so it's well worth your time to investigate everything LinkedIn has to offer you. Your starting point should be http://nonprofits.linkedin.com.

Visually Appealing Platforms:
If your business or organization lends itself well to promoting with photos or videos, make sure you check out the platforms that thrive on visuals. Those platforms include Pinterest, Instagram and YouTube. All three of these platforms enable you to share your photography, follow others, share their content, and gather back-end statistics regarding engagement. And, let's not forget that YouTube is currently the #2 online search engine after Google!

And there you have it: your business is officially part of the social media world. Success on social media may not happen overnight. Remember: It's about engagement and dialogue. Show the human side of your organization and the people behind it. Use photos and videos to capture you and your employees in action. You might even have some fun creating a Meme with a photo editor like Picmonkey or Canva! A meme, as defined in Wikipedia, is "An idea, behavior, or style that spreads from person to person within a culture. An Internet meme may take the form of an image, hyperlink, video, picture, website, or hashtag." Who knows, maybe your Meme will even go viral?

Internet Domain Presence (Your Website)
Your Address in Cyberspace

You need a landing page. Even if your location services and social media strategies are designed to drive followers and fans to a physical business location, you still need a digital location for those who need more information before they make the trip to your storefront. If you are a service provider who does not operate from a single location, this is all the more reason to provide potential clients with a way to "visit" your business.

You may envision a relatively simple website, but think through whether or not you want to tackle this task on your own (remember my advice from Chapter One). Although there are a number of user-friendly free or low-cost website building platforms out there, you may still need to contend with a learning curve and a time commitment that would draw too much of your attention away from what is most important: building your business.

Whichever path you choose, a quick search on Google will turn up thousands of resources. It is easy to find detailed user reviews of website building platforms, such as Wordpress and Wix. Once you choose a platform, help sites and user blogs are plentiful. If you decide to hire a professional website designer, a general internet search will make it easy to locate thousands of designers who specialize in creating beautiful and functional sites. Don't hesitate to contact other professionals whose websites you admire or members of your local Chamber for recommendations on website designers. You will have a lot of decisions to make about structure, color, content and design, as well as functionality, and I hope you have fun with the process. Here are *my* tips for getting the most out of the little piece of real estate that you stake out as your own:

- Clearly identify the problem you solve, and how you solve it.

- Include a brief bio and photographs of key staff. If yours is a nonprofit organization, include information about staff and also the board of trustees or directors. People want to get to know the people behind the business or organization.

- Make sure that all of your social media platforms point to your website...and that every page of your website includes links to all of your social media platforms. This is easy to address by putting the icons in the header or footer of your web pages.

- Once you get visitors to your website, offer them something for free in return for signing up for your mailing list. A coupon or a free consultation, or some sort of how-to guide that relates to the problem that your business solves. You can attach it to a welcome email. The goal is to get permission to deliver content, such as your newsletter and other announcements, to their email in-box.

- Make the e-news opt-in and contact forms available on every page of the site, not just the home page.

- Make sure that your site is mobile responsive. People use their phones and tablets as much as, and sometimes more than, their desktop or laptop computers. Google search results now favor mobile-responsive sites. Remember, people searching on a small screen will not be able to read tiny text. A minimum of 11 point font, please!

- Consider including some video. This can be clips from a celebration event or workshop, a guided tour of your shop or facility, or testimonials from happy clients. Animoto (animoto.com) offers a free version of their software that makes it easy to put together a polished video from your photos—including a few special effects! If your budget allows, however, I highly recommend hiring a professional videographer to showcase your business. When Google purchased YouTube, YouTube became the number two search engine on the planet. Without video, you are blind to the second most used search engine.

- Don't skimp on testing. Check out how your site looks and functions on a variety of browsers and devices. Optimizely (www.optimizely.com) offers a free version of its landing page testing and optimization service to help you ensure that you are getting the most out of your website. At https://developers.google.com/webmasters/

mobile-sites/get-started/?hl=en, Google Developers offers a free test to find out if your website is mobile friendly. To reiterate, in April 2015, Google announced that, in essence, if your website is not mobile-responsive, it won't show up on Google results served on mobile devices. Currently, over 60% of Google searches are done on mobile devices and that figure will certainly grow steadily! Don't miss this opportunity to be found.

Google constantly changes its algorithms. One of their changes involved how they rank websites. Now, sites are ranked based on how much educational, informational, non-selling, fresh content appears on your site. You can no longer "fool" the search engine with coding and tagging alone to increase your ranking.

If you are still a little put off by the idea of developing and maintaining a full website *and* you like to write, consider launching a WordPress blog. WordPress is free, but you will still need to purchase and register a domain name and take the time to select and customize a template. This will give you a one-page, interactive web page with your own web address to include in your social media pages and on your business cards. Each new blog post becomes content for your social media pages as well.

The Care and Feeding of Your Online Presence

The Internet is a dynamic and ever-evolving universe, and so your presence there needs to be dynamic and responsive too. On the other hand, you don't want to be spending all day, every day tending to your social media accounts and website, right? Here are a few tips to help keep you on top of your online marketing without drowning in tweets, posts and updates:

- First, establish a schedule for posting. Remember Ryan Pinkham's advice, earlier in this chapter, regarding differences in frequency demanded by each of your platforms. You might decide to tweet daily, but limit Facebook updates to once weekly, and website blog posts to once or twice a month.

- Make it easy to find great content worth sharing. The RSS feeds we discussed in Chapter One are a great place to start.

Shareist.com, Feedly.com® and Flipboard are great free services that help you locate and share content that will be beneficial to your audience, and it has built-in tools for measuring traffic and conversion. These services allow you to customize your experience, so you will always get the topics that are most interesting to you. Just make sure you don't share anything that requires a subscription or registration. You don't want to risk frustrating your readers.

- Survey results make great content too, and can be packaged in interesting ways. Google offers an Infographics Toolbox and other sites, such as Piktochart.com, help you build custom infographics for free.

- Recycle your content across your platforms, but do so thoughtfully. Remember the nuances of tone, length and frequency, and how these things change from platform to platform.

> *"Become the 'Bigfoot', with a magnified online presence…and become more searchable."*

It might be helpful to think of your online presence as an in-depth calling card, a way to tell and show the scope, quality, and value of your work. Once you've taken the time to create a website and social media sites, consider how this plays into your overall "digital footprint". Consider if there are businesses or nonprofits who are complementary to your own who would be willing to place your logo on their own websites and back-link to your website. This strategy works well with blogs, too. If you are a guest blogger on someone else's blog, make sure there is a link back to your own blog or website. All of these strategies will help with your company's Search Engine Optimization (SEO).

Keep in mind that your website is just a part of your online presence, as is your social media. People that do not already know you, your company name or your website address (URL) have a better chance of finding you if you have more content in more places online, that links back to you. Remember, they are searching for information on your *subject matter*. The more valuable content you have around the web on other sites, the better their chance of discovering you and visiting your site. Consider contributing content to sites such as the International Expert Directory (www.internationalexpertdirectory.com), or responding to queries on Mosaic Hub (www.mosaichub.com). If you have achieved expert status in your field, you may even want to serve as an expert witness for legal cases. You can respond to media inquiries via HARO (Help A Reporter Out) which results in having other people write about or quote you. Register at www.haro.com. You can list yourself with Thomson Reuters' Westlaw Roundtable Group of Expert Witnesses (www.theexpertnetworks.com/westlaw-round-table-group). Some trade associations also have resource directories for their members on their websites, as well. All of these listings will make you more searchable and add to your perceived value as an expert in your field.

Every social media platform provides space for a photograph, and your website should include one too. Not only should you be sure to include a photo (an empty head shot space gives the impression that you just don't care enough to include one), but make sure it is a good one. Here are some tips:

- If you can, have a professional photo taken. It doesn't have to be an expensive photo shoot by a fashion photographer; your local department store studio can provide a high-resolution image on a DVD for under $100.

- Wear clothing appropriate to your business. Unless it is the holiday rush season, most studios will allow a quick wardrobe change so you can bring an extra jacket, tie, or blouse with you. Ladies, go easy on the accessories.

- Ladies, consider spending a few more dollars on having a professional blow-out at the salon. Gentlemen, a quick haircut and professional shave are a good idea.

- Go easy on the re-touching. It Is tempting to have the studio take ten years off your face, but the goal of the photo is to represent the genuine you. Anyone who looks at your photograph should be able to recognize you in person.

- Update your photo every few years.

Chapter Four: In-Person Networking

Online marketing tools are wonderful for initiating contact, and for opening and sustaining a dialogue. At their best, however, they are part of a larger marketing strategy that includes in-person networking. Yes, that's what I said: put down the smart phone and get out there to shake a few hands, look into a few eyes... and flash a few smiles.

My in-person networking advice comes in two parts: where to go, and what to do once you get there.

Where to Network

Think about whom and where you serve. If you intend to serve your local geographic region, there are a number of opportunities for getting out there to meet people. Your local **chamber of commerce** can connect you to the other business owners in your area, a valuable network even if you are running a nonprofit organization.

Clubs and associations exist for just about every profession, interest, or hobby that you can think of. The Gale *Encyclopedia of Associations* is available at many libraries. It is huge and consists of several volumes, but I am sure the reference librarian can help you to get the most out of this resource. This publication is also available through most public libraries as a searchable online database that you can access through your library card.

First, you will want to look into associations that are directly related to your field. For example, if you are a financial planner, you may want to join your area's chapter of the Financial Planning Association®. Fundraising professionals will want to join the Association of Fundraising Professionals. Get the most out of your membership fee by attending workshops and conferences to keep up on the latest trends while also networking with your peers. Serving on committees places you elbow to elbow with people you want to meet—and demonstrates that you are committed to helping the organization accomplish its mission.

"Network with allied professionals to your field."

Be creative in your approach as well, and consider allied professions and interests. For example, as a financial planner you might want to find ways to meet up with the CPAs and estate planning attorneys in your neighborhood. A fundraising professional who specializes in planned giving might benefit from the same strategy. Most associations have membership fees and event registration charges, but many also allow non-members to attend workshops and networking events for a slightly elevated registration charge. This is a great way to check out whether an association is a good fit for you and your business before you invest in annual membership dues.

Conference admission can be pricey, so here's an insider's tip: find out if there are opportunities to volunteer at the event in return for a reduced or waived conference fee. It may mean showing up extra early as a greeter, or staying late to collect attendee surveys, but both of those scenarios offer additional networking opportunities on top of the waived fee. Better yet, if you are comfortable with public speaking, respond to their call for presenters and you will likely get that conference fee waived. Speaking at conferences is a great way to elevate your profile and stature within your industry and generally helps you to stand out from the crowd. Consider attending trade shows and conferences in your *prospective clients'* industries, not just your own field.

When was the last time you contacted your **alumni association**? Even if you don't live near your alma mater, schools have regional chapters. A quick search of the school website and LinkedIn will often tell you whether there is one in your area. If you still aren't sure, a call to the central alumni relations office can point you in the right direction. No chapter in your area? Offer to help start one. Alumni relations departments are always looking for volunteers and will likely be happy to search their database for other graduates in your area, and to help you get going. Once again, check LinkedIn for alumni groups for your alma mater…or consider starting one.

So far I've mentioned two ways to use **volunteering** as a way to build your person-to-person network. Here is a third: if you are very new to your profession, offer to practice your skills for a local nonprofit organization. For example, if you want to break into public relations or grant writing, see if there is a local nonprofit who needs help in these areas. Offer your services in return for referrals and recommendations. Just remember to treat this relationship with the same regard, and boundaries, as you would a paying client.

If you are civic-minded, take a look at your local **civic organizations**, such as Rotary Clubs, Lions Clubs and Kiwanis®. These organizations often have strict requirements regarding attendance, volunteer participation, financial contributions and promoting your own business within the group, so it is important to know what you are getting into. On the other hand, they generally have a generous get-to-know process so you have a chance to learn the protocols fully before you make a decision to join.

Formal networking groups exist, and maybe that's the route for you. BNI International® (www.bni.com) and LeTip International (www.letip.com) offer significant in-person and online networking. You could also start your own networking group. Meetup (www.meetup.com) is free, and offers about as many opportunities to think creatively as a person could want. For example, the owner of a frozen yogurt shop in my neighborhood offered his store as a location for a mom-and-toddler Meetup group. He chose a time that was typically slow for his business, and offered free yogurt to the tots. A dog groomer might join a puppy playgroup (making sure, of course, that her puppy looked *fabulous* for every visit) as a way to highlight her business.

What to Do When You Get There

For many (most?) of us, the idea of walking into a room full of strangers takes us right back to our middle school cafeteria experiences. It helps to remember that everyone else probably feels the same way. It also helps to prepare.

A great read for networking newbies and seasoned networkers alike is Andrea Nierenberg's *Million Dollar Networking: The Sure Way to Find, Grow and Keep Your Business.* Her website, www.nierenberggroup.com, has several other book suggestions and a blog worth checking out. She breaks networking down into manageable steps and offers strategies to help you overcome your discomfort. Introverts need not worry: Andrea points out that introverts have a keen sense of listening that is vital to building relationships, even work-related ones. As an extrovert, my own challenge is to stay focused on what the other person is saying before I jump in with my ideas.

In many ways, the work you did in the previous three chapters was preparation for your in-person networking. By now you should have such a good handle on your USP that it rolls off your tongue in one smooth statement. If you're not quite there yet, it doesn't hurt to practice—out loud and in front of a mirror, and face to face with family and friends specifically recruited for the purpose. Learn to have clear conversations about your business. Learn to deliver your message as a value proposition, rather than just an "elevator speech." Tell people how you help solve problems; don't give them an inventory of every product or service you provide.

"Your first goal is to build credibility and trust."

But what, you may ask, comes after the value proposition or elevator speech? Good question, and an important one too. Business relationships are about much more than your best pitch. What you do next will define your brand on a whole new level, so make sure that your in-person approach is consistent with what you have created online. Your first goal is to build credibility and trust, and there is a very fine line between networking for business purposes and being too sales-y. Show up, listen first, give first, ask for what you need and set up one-on-one meetings over coffee to learn more about possible synergies with your companies. Most important of all, do what you say you will do. Follow up; send that email; make that introduction.

People who walk into an event with the sole purpose of collecting as many business cards as possible and then hammering this new "audience" with a pitch give networking a bad name. If the event organizer lists attendees on their event page, this is an opportunity to do some research in advance of the event to know who will be there and figure out a strategy for connecting with them at the event. You can even find and connect with them on LinkedIn prior to the event, letting them know you are looking forward to meeting in person.

Here are three strategies for starting a new relationship off on solid ground:

- **I can help with that**. Pay attention to what your conversation-mates are saying, and look for opportunities to be of assistance. It may have little to do with your actual business—maybe they just want to know of a good Thai restaurant in the area—but the exchange offers an opportunity to continue a conversation via email. And of course your email signature includes links to your website and social media profiles, right?

- **I know someone who can help with that.** Be a connector. Offer to facilitate an in-person or online introduction. The referrals you make will come back to you many times over in the form of goodwill. Check back with both parties later to gauge whether or not the referred service reflected your standards—you can't control third party relationships, but you should be thoughtful about those you recommend.

- **Can I get more information about that?** You don't want to reach out to a stranger for the sole purpose of picking his or her brain, but it doesn't hurt to ask them to email you a link to a website or news article of interest, or the name and author of a book that they mentioned. Return the favor with a gracious thank you via phone, email or even a handwritten note.

Your commitment to following through on these offers is critical. Do what you offered to do in as timely a manner as possible. This will distinguish you as someone who can be trusted as a potential service provider and business partner. This is what polishes your brand.

Conferences and local networking events are great for concentrated networking, but they can be expensive when you add up registration fees, travel and hotel costs if it lasts more than one day. If you decide to make the investment, here are some tips for getting the most out of the experience:

- Before you even walk through the doors, make sure you have a mindset of openness, and of service to others. Don't let your frame of mind cloud what you can potentially get out of the day. Do what you need to do to show up as your best self. Ask yourself: What can I learn today? How might I help someone else today?

- Make sure your appearance reflects how you want to be remembered. You never have a second chance to make a first impression. Study how other successful professionals in your field dress for inspiration.

- Have an ample supply of nice quality business cards that include all the ways to

Magnify Your Business

contact you—phone, email, LinkedIn profile URL. While you're at it, why not create a customized LinkedIn URL? On the "Edit My Public Profile" page, you can create a custom URL for your public profile. If the front of your card is looking too busy, make good use of the real estate on the back of the card.

- Every conference issues name tags. If you want to stand out, have a magnetic tag made at your local trophy shop that reflects your website color scheme and includes your logo.

- Place your name tag on your right lapel. Every time you reach out to shake hands with someone, their eye will be drawn naturally to it.

- Practice your hand shake—not too limp, not bone crushing—and look people in the eyes when you meet them.

- Do what you can to remember names. Help your memory along by repeating it during the conversation. (Bob, what did you get out of the last workshop session? Jennifer, how did you learn about this conference?). If you run into that person again and just can't remember the name, it's okay to apologize and ask again. For all you know, they forgot your name too.

- You are spending precious time and money to attend a conference, so don't spend all of your time talking to people you already know. True, it is fun to catch up with old friends, but it is important to bring new friends into the fold. If you are feeling bold, go ahead and walk up to a small group and introduce yourself. If that is too intimidating, find another lone soul and make your own group. Chances are good that this person will be deeply grateful for your effort!

- Time to break away from a group? To excuse yourself, let them know how much you enjoyed meeting them but you know that they want to meet others as well. If you need to move on from a one-to-one conversation, find an opportunity to introduce your counterpart to someone else, someone that you know or have recently met, and then excuse yourself. Again, put yourself in the connector role.

- Mind your manners with food and drink.

- Have a working pen with you. When you are making plans to contact someone in the future, ask what their preferred method of communication is and note it on the back of their business card.

- If it is a multi-day conference, set up opportunities to network over dinner. Some conference organizers make this easy with sign-up sheets for specific restaurants. The group may even include a person from the sponsoring association who is assigned as ambassador for the evening.

- It is common for participants to leave conferences early, especially if it is a one-day conference. You may need to do so as well, but if you can spare the extra time consider the value of networking in a quieter environment.

- After the conference, make sure you deliver on any offers you made to provide information or introductions. Whether or not you've promised anything, you might still extend an invitation to connect via LinkedIn. Make the invitation personal, with an invitation to visit your website and opt-in for your e-news or blog mailing list.

- Consider offering your services as a panel speaker at future conferences. While you won't be paid for your time, it is a great way to establish yourself as an expert in your field.

Meaningful business relationships are about more than what your business provides; they are about the value and contributions that you, as a business professional, bring to the table. No one understands this better than Andrea Nierenberg, author of four books on networking and President of Nierenberg Consulting Group. In one of her blog posts, Andrea advises:

Pulling It All Together

You meet people and have the opportunity to network anyplace, anytime. Networking is a "nonstop" process; it is just living your life, connecting with people, learning, giving and making things happen. Often the word is very misunderstood. In fact some people give up on networking because they think it is only about handing out business cards, asking for referrals and immediately getting something. Nothing could be further from the truth. Building the relationships you need in order to reach your potential is easier than you think, yet it does take work. Look at it as a simple five-step process.

1. Meet people. Welcome opportunities to meet new people, and re-connect with those you already know. Have a 24/7 awareness and curiosity about what you learn from each person you connect with.

2. Listen and learn. Everybody likes to talk and often about themselves. When you listen, you will learn who they are, what is important to them, how you can help them, and how they might possibly help you.

3. Make connections. Help people connect with others you know who could help them and perhaps create a new synergy.

4. Follow up. When you promise to do something, make it happen, and do it in a timely manner. Follow-up is one of the golden keys of authentic networking.

5. Stay in touch. After an initial period of contact, if nothing happens, most people will just move on. Here is where a networking system really "works" for successful networkers. Successful networkers find ways to stay in touch and continue to build relationships. Why? Because their goal is to build a network of long-lasting, mutually beneficial relationships, not just to get an immediate "result."

Bonus take away from opportunities that result from a Networking connection:

1. Learn something from the other person
2. Give something back- a suggestion or piece of advice or information
3. Take something away- perhaps a reason for a follow up meeting
4. Implement your follow up strategy with a date and time.

I recommend visiting Andrea's site at http://www.nierenberggroup.com. You can subscribe to The Nierenblog at http://www.nierenberggroup.com/about/nierenblog.

Chapter Five:
Harnessing the Power of Email Marketing

You now have all the ingredients of a great marketing campaign. Your digital presence is looking great. You have current profiles up on at least three social media platforms, and all include a professional-looking photo of you as well as your logo. It is easy to connect from each of them to your website's home page, which also features your logo. You are ready for face-to-face networking too, with branded business cards and name tag, and a positive, professional approach to meeting new people. Your USP is clear and consistent from Facebook page to website to conversation. It's time to flip the switch!

Why email?

Email marketing is a powerful business-building tool. Your email list is a valuable asset. In fact, it is recognized as such by the United States government through the Federal Trade Commission's CAN-SPAM Act (https://www.ftc.gov/tips-advice/business-center/guidance/

can-spam-act-compliance-guide-business), which requires that we treat our customer lists with great respect. If there is a chance that you will do business in Canada, be sure to familiarize yourself with the Canadian Radio-television and Telecommunications Commission's Anti-Spam Legislation (http://www.crtc.gc.ca/eng/casl-lcap.htm). It is important to comply with the laws governing your business; it is also important to do all you can to build a good reputation. At its core, email marketing is about permission-based marketing. Nobody wants to be known as a "spammer."

Research confirms the value of email marketing. In its 50 Email Marketing Tips and Stats for 2014, ExactTarget.com reported that, "Marketers received an average return on investment of $44.25 for every $1 spent on email marketing." Another study, this one by MarketingProfs.com, found email to be the preferred communication channel for one-third of consumers. Email marketing is an opportunity to deliver your marketing messages directly to your customers' in boxes, and to be part of a flow of information that they are highly likely to review on at least a daily basis.

Those of you managing nonprofit organizations have additional regulations to consider. Many states require that any organization raising funds within its borders register annually with the attorney general's office. So if your appeal crosses state lines, you need to make sure you have filed the appropriate paperwork. If you're not sure how to do this, check out Tony Martignetti's book, *Charity Registration: State-by-State Guidelines for Compliance*. Information is available on his website http://www.tonymartignetti.com.

You should also check out the Association of Fundraising Professionals' Donor Bill of Rights. Information is available through their website http://www.afpnet.org. Organizations such as Kimbia are now considering a crowdfunder bill of rights as well (http://www.kimbia.com/need-feedback-crowdfunder-bill-rights/).

> ***"Email marketing is a one-to-one digital conversation with people who have opted in to receive your communications"***

The procedures that you will follow to comply with all of these regulations will also ensure that your list is the asset that you want it to be: *a compilation of your ideal clients or people who can refer you to your ideal clients.* Social media platforms are wonderful, but the truth is that you don't "own" your followers. If a platform suddenly disappeared, your followers would go with it. And while social media builds a sense of community, email marketing is a one-to-one digital conversation with *your* people—those who have gone from social media follower or conference lunch-mates to potential clients *who have opted in specifically to receive your communications.*

From this perspective, then, your chief marketing strategy is to provide as many opportunities as you can, and to make it as easy and rewarding as possible, for potential customers to join your list. All of your social media profiles already link to your website's home page, so make sure that your home page includes an opt-in field in the header or sidebar. Even better, include the opt-in field as a template element so that it appears on *every* page in your website.

Your face-to-face networking is another opportunity to invite potential clients to join your list. The information they will need to do so is right on your business card, and you can always follow up with an emailed invitation. You can always add a hyperlinked "invitation to join" to your email signature, in addition to the other live links you provide. Just make sure you provide a one-click opportunity to opt out.

This is where your email service provider comes in. There are a number of email service providers available, at different price points (including a few that are free if your list is small) and pricing structures, from pay-as-you-go to subscription arrangements. Some will offer a free trial period so you can test the service before you buy. Since the purpose of these applications is to manage email marketing, built-in opt-in/opt-out functions will ensure compliance with spam regulations. But there are other features to think about as well. And considering what we know is the value of your contact list, be sure you read the reviews and choose the best platform you can afford. Questions to ask include:

- How easy is it to set up the system?
- How easy is it to create and send an email?
- How easy is it to change the look of my email, so that it reflects my brand?
- Can I segment my list?
- What kind of automated features are available? Can I schedule communications in advance?

- What kind of analytics will be available to me?

- What kind of tech support is available if I should have a problem?

- Will they keep me compliant with anti-spam laws by providing one-click opt-out opportunities to subscribers?

These apps are designed to support your email marketing strategy. When you open an account, the app generates a small bit of code that gets inserted into your website template that shows up in your website as an invitation to join your list. Depending on the app and your subscription level, you will have choices about how the invitation looks, and what information you can capture from each new subscriber. Once someone enters their information they will receive an opt-in confirmation email. Once they click "confirm," their information loads into your contact list.

As with anything else, you get what you pay for. Fortunately, there are robust online communities surrounding all things technological and these can help you evaluate your choices. This is another instance when you might want to ask fellow professionals or organizations about the services that they use, and what they think of their experience.

> *"It's much better to have someone opt out than to click the spam button."*

I know it sounds like a lot of work to build a list from scratch, but please resist the temptation to purchase and upload a "starter" list. I can't speak for every email service provider out there, but as a Constant Contact Master Certified Solution Provider, I can tell you that Constant Contact is very strict about spam reports and will block your activity and request a phone conversation about the issue if they deem it necessary. Although no one ever wants to lose a subscriber, it's much better to have someone opt out than to click the spam button: opt-out information is made available to you, while spam clicks are anonymous.

Email services are powerful tools that can be tailored to your marketing strategy. Yes, they require time and attention on your part, but you will be pleasantly surprised at how much can be automated so that your marketing program is working for you while you are working on other things. Below I list some of the ways that I use my email service system. Just remember that I use a paid subscription with Constant Contact; if you choose another service, you will need to find out if it offers the same or a similar feature.

- I use the email feature to introduce a new blog topic. The email includes just a few opening sentences and a live link to the full blog, which—of course—includes social media "share" buttons.

- In addition to blog posts, I can email notifications about upcoming events and speaking engagements. I can schedule these notices at various points prior to the event, each with a slightly different message and all with a link to the event registration page.

- When someone opts in to my list, they will receive a pre-set series of welcome communications, each with a different bit of information, such as tips and resources, that I think they will find useful.

- Constant Contact offers a text-to-join feature. When I am speaking to a group, I can invite them to text right then and there to join my subscriber list. This enables me to grow my list before I've even left the podium.

I encourage you to use automated services whenever possible. They are huge timesavers. Just make sure you are offering something useful and not too sales-y. You don't want to encourage people to opt out. You may have heard of the 80/20 rule. In sales, it goes something like this: 80% of your revenue will result from 20% of your customers. The same holds true for email marketing: if you can provide something of value to your email subscribers 80% of the time, they will tolerate being sold to 20% of the time. In fact, this is a great rule of thumb for your social media efforts, too.

Automation isn't limited to email marketing, either. There are several services—Hootsuite™ and Buffer are two—that allow you to manage your social networks. Hootsuite is free for up to three social networks. It allows you to pre-set and time your posts. This is another useful tool in the lead-up to an event, conference, or speaking engagement. You can create different post content, images and timing for each network so that your posts are appropriate to each channel. The free version of Buffer allows a maximum limit of ten posts to be scheduled at any given time, and allows management of only one social media account per social media website. Both services offer subscriptions that provide additional features.

Chapter Six:
Prospecting Strategies to Build Your List

In-person networking and getting your message out via social media may be enough to feed your particular business. Then again, you might be feeling the need to fuel your efforts in a bigger way. If that's the case, I have two incredibly useful resources that are available to you at little or no cost.

It's the Latest, it's the Greatest, it's the Library

Public libraries offer free access to numerous databases, most of which would be very expensive to access on your own. Some libraries even offer remote access as long as you have a valid library card, and a local library card will likely grant you access to your county and statewide library system. If you aren't sure where to start, you can begin by visiting www.publiclibraries.com, which organizes libraries by state. The site also provides links to college and university libraries. Each institution will have policies about non-student use, but many will welcome on-site and remote use by alumni.

My favorite library resource for business prospecting is *ReferenceUSA®*, a collection of searchable databases that include millions of U.S. and Canadian businesses, corporate executives and healthcare professionals. The *ReferenceUSA* consumer databases include nearly 90 million households in the U.S. and another 12 million in Canada. It is an extremely valuable resource and it is available to you to generate targeted prospect lists for your business or nonprofit organization.

So let's combine the idea of a searchable database with your definition of the ideal client. Perhaps you have created and would like to market a high-end skin cream. Your ideal customer might be spas that cater to upscale clientele. You could use *ReferenceUSA* to identify spa businesses in specific geographic areas, sorting by state, county, zip code, or even neighborhood. You might want to narrow that list to include only those with a certain minimum number of employees, and those that generate a certain minimum revenue level. You could then export those business names, along with addresses, phone numbers and executive names, into a spreadsheet. *Voila!* You now have an entire list of businesses that fit your description of an ideal client.

As the skin cream marketer, you might want to plan a mailing to those businesses that includes a small sample of your product. Or you might want to visit some or all of them to deliver a sample in person, or spend some time cold calling by phone. However you choose to reach out, you can rest assured that your investment of time and money is targeting the audience you most want to attract. I can't think of a better deal for entrepreneurs and start-ups, since you can access the database for free with your library card.

ReferenceUSA can be just as useful for nonprofit organizations. I once used it to help the Women's Leadership Council of United Way of Northern New Jersey expand the audience for its annual spring fundraising breakfast. Our goal was to attract women executives in a particular New Jersey county. I searched for female managers of companies within our geographic target area. I narrowed the list by selected companies that reported a minimum annual revenue and minimum number of employees. While the list I generated incurred additional mailing costs, the effort resulted in a new $500 sponsor in the first year alone.

I *do not* recommend email as a strategy for contacting people or businesses on *ReferenceUSA* lists. First, know that while mailing address, phone number and contact name lists are available from *ReferenceUSA* at no cost, the company does charge for generating lists of email addresses. Second, remember my advice about dumping large lists of contacts into your email service provider account. *You don't want to build a reputation as a spammer!* Instead, plan to invest your time (or that of a relative or friend) in making phone calls or visits. If the list is too large for that, consider spending a few dollars developing a postcard with a QR code that recipients can scan with their phones to visit your home page. Services such as Vistaprint.com are easy to use and budget-friendly.

ReferenceUSA is just one benefit of using the library system. Another wonderful resource is the reference librarian. These professionals can direct you to the best resources and tell you which ones are available remotely and which require a visit to the library. They can also help you get the most out of the resources you choose to use. Most will provide assistance over the phone during business hours, and some libraries even offer free online chat services outside business hours. The New York Public Library (www.nypl.org) even has a 24/7 chat line that is open to non-members. Better yet, the service will email you a transcript of your session that includes any links that were recommended and instructions provided.

Any time, anywhere access might not seem like a priority, but if you travel at all for business it can be a real time saver. For example, say that a flight change or appointment cancellation leaves you with a lengthy stretch of additional hours in a particular city. You could access *ReferenceUSA* or another database to identify other potential businesses to visit. Once you secure a meeting, reference libraries and the professionals who run them can help you prepare, providing information about finances, products, markets, current developments and more, so that your first face-to-face meeting will leave a great impression.

> *"LinkedIn is the only mine-able social media platform...free"*

The second resource I highly recommend is LinkedIn. I know I have mentioned this platform several times in previous chapters, but as things stand, it is the only mine-able social media platform. Clicking the word "Advanced," right next to the search box at the top of the page, allows you to search within your first- and second-degree networks, from your groups, or more broadly from the entire

LinkedIn database. Other search fields include industry, company, title, school, nonprofit interests, and language. A text field allows you to add key words into the mix.

It gets better. Not only will the LinkedIn free version allow you to save up to three searches, it will update them weekly or monthly (your choice) and send the results to you via email. Prospecting does not get easier—or more automated—than that! As of the writing of this book, all of this is available with your free LinkedIn membership! Additional refinements are offered with the paid premium membership.

Once you have your list, you can plot your strategy. For second-degree links, you can request an introduction. For prospects a little more removed, you can still send a personalized connection request.

I hope you will leverage these tools to your advantage. Sure, there will be times when you feel like you don't have the answers that you need. But now you know that there is an outsourced research team available to you, as long as you have a valid library card, a free LinkedIn account and a bookmark to the New York Public Library reference page.

Magnify Your Business

My Top 10 Tips to Grow Your Email List:

1. If you have a brick-and-mortar business, collect business cards in a 'fish bowl' or set out a sign-in book. Make it clear that they'll become part of your V.I.P. Community, sharing in special deals.

2. Include a sign-up form on every page of your website. You can even offer some sort of freebie or coupon in order to entice that sign-up and they'll receive value from you right away! Keep your sign-up form short and only ask for the information you absolutely need. You can always collect more information down the line from your subscribers.

3. Make it simple for your Facebook fans to join your list by adding a sign-up form to your Facebook page. (If you're using Constant Contact, you'll create this form from within your Constant Contact account, not through Facebook.)

4. Let your followers on your blog and all your social media platforms know that they can get your important news delivered directly into their inboxes. Occasionally remind them by providing the link to your sign-up form.

5. Put a sign-up link in your e-newsletter! Seems counterintuitive, right? But, consider this: Many people will forward and share your email on social media, so people who aren't subscribed yet will have access to reading it. So, make it as simple as possible for them to sign up, too!

6. Remember to include a hyperlink in your email's automated signature line. This way, your one-on-one communications with your customers and new prospects will have a one-click access to subscribing to your list. Be careful, however, not to list too many links or jpeg images in your signature line, since it can trigger a spam alert and route you to their spam box instead of their in box.

7. Use "Text to Join" feature included with your Constant Contact account to allow people to easily sign up to your list by using their smartphones! Example: When someone texts the word "Prospect" to the number 22828, they'll receive a text back asking them for their email address. Once they reply back with their email address, then they're automatically added to my database and I haven't lifted a finger! This feature is great if you are a speaker or if you exhibit at trade shows and conferences. It is super simple to set up, so don't forget to do this.

Magnify Your Business

8. Have an iPad? Use the iCapture tool to allow people to sign themselves up as you are out networking and attending conferences.

9. Remember to include information on your printed materials! Either direct them to your website to sign up or else implement the Text to Join feature.

10. If you run events, provide an opportunity to sign up through the online registration form they're filling out for your event.

Chapter Seven: If only I Had an App for That... Resources to Get the Most Out of Your Time

We all have the same 24 hours in the day. Once you become an entrepreneur, those hours will probably seem shorter than ever! Take heart: technology offers a lot of free and low-cost tools that can help you to get the most out of every one of those hours.

Conferencing and Meeting Tools

First, you might want to check with your phone provider to see if your plan already includes a conference calling service or feature. It may be that you already have a conferencing resource at your fingertips and ready to go!

In Chapter 2, I touched on several free conferencing services as tools that you can use to set up cost- and time-conscious focus groups. Let's take another look at how these same tools can save you time and boost productivity, without draining your company's budget.

- As I mentioned, **FreeConferencePro** (http://www.freeconferencepro.com) enables you to host up to 200 people on a free conference call, and has a recording feature that enables you to share the recording afterward. This is useful for off-site meetings with employees and far-flung subcontractors; it is also a great tool for meetings with clients. With a recording of your conversation, you never have to worry about neglecting a client's request or concern.

- **GoToMeeting** (http://www.gotomeeting.com) by Citrix, the service I mentioned that offers a free version allowing up to three people to participate in an online meeting, has webcam and screen sharing features. This is extremely useful for collaborative projects, and also for training sessions. Meetings can be recorded as well, so that your training session becomes a personalized video tutorial for your client to review and use after the training session. Hosting more than three people requires a subscription. Another alternative is **Adobe Connect** (http://www.adobe.com/products/adobeconnect.html). This fee-based service, which offers a free trial period, offers a more robust platform for meetings, conferences, and training. **Webex** is similar, with pricing based on the number of people who attend your meetings; it is free for up to three participants.

- The free face-to-face online meetings at **Google Hangouts** (https://plus.google.com/hangouts) lets you and other users who have a free Google account to "hang out" online. You can publicize upcoming "hang outs" via your e-newsletter and social media, and then use the time to get to know new potential clients. You can even build a little goodwill by providing free mini-webinars. Hangouts can be public or private and can be recorded and shared via **Hangouts On Air**, or uploaded to your YouTube channel. **MeetMe.com** and **Join.me** are additional free, mobile-friendly chat services.

- **Skype** (http://www.skype.com/en/), the service that started it all, remains free, easy to use, and useful for online face-to-face meetings with staff, sub-contractors, or clients. **Facetime** provides a similar function that works well for teams that are using Apple products.

Most services now offer desktop and mobile versions, so that you can get a lot done even when you are on the move. Many also have a free version with limited capability, or at least offer a free trial period so you can test the service before you invest in it. Just be sure to check the pricing tabs and compare prices and features carefully.

With so many tools available, the possibilities extend as far as the imagination can take you. Meetings can be "face-to-face," or focus on a slide presentation, or incorporate both. They can be active, allowing an instructor or team leader to walk participants through live Internet or application maneuvers. They can be interactive, allowing one or more team members to alter a document or project as the conversation develops. And all of this can be accomplished with zero travel time and cost.

Technology is removing the geographic limitations of business. Several years ago, I worked on a project that involved several team members from across Alaska, and I never left New Jersey! For a small business owner who is selling a product, say a handcrafted item that is personalized for each order, this kind of technology can help to achieve a higher level of customer satisfaction.

Nonprofits can reach higher with technology as well. Consider Orbis International, which uses teleconferencing to provide eye health training to medical professionals in developing countries around the world. Charity:water uses videos and tutorials to provide step-by-step instructions to donors who want to help raise funds for the organization. Room to Read relies on communication technologies to coordinate its work with communities and local governments to put books into the hands of children across Asia and Africa.

Productivity and Management Tools

Once upon a time, sticky notes were the way to go when it came to jotting down notes and ideas. That was when I spent most of my days at a single location; today, I'm on the run more than I am at my desk, and I'm betting that this is the case for many business professionals, entrepreneurs and nonprofit executives. Frankly, I prefer to be on the road, but that means I need extra help keeping track of new information and creative inspirations. Here are a few tools that are worth exploring:

- **Evernote.com** is about as complete a digital workspace as one could imagine. You can type in notes, pull clips from the web, upload photos, and even dictate using the app's speech-to-text feature. Through Evernote.com's business card scan capability you can shorten your turnaround time when reaching out to new contacts via email or LinkedIn. You can share your Evernote space with your team to make sure everyone is on the same page. The search function helps to ensure that important notes and ideas are never lost.

- **Pocket.com®** is a short-term bookmarking app that captures articles from your browser or from other apps, such as Flipboard or Pulse, and lets you read them even when you don't have access to the Internet. It's a great way to get the most out of your commuting time.

- **Basecamp** and **Asana** are apps designed specifically for managing collaborative group projects. These are the tools to use to keep your team on track, while keeping email to a minimum. If collaborating on a large document or powerpoint, it will neatly keep everything in one place where the team can add edits and feedback. Gone is the need to search your inbox for the conversation stream.

- The **IF** app by IFTTT (If This Then That) uses "recipes" to keep your business streamlined. For example, emails from your accountant could be automatically directed to your Evernote folder for financial management.

- Cloud storage, such as **Google Drive, DropBox** and **OneDrive** allow teams to share documents and presentations and are especially useful for sharing large files that are likely to exceed email size limits. I also use cloud storage for presentation materials for speaking engagements, as a backup in case I forget to bring my flash drive!

Tools to Corral Drains on Your Personal Time

There are a lot of tools that can help to streamline other aspects of your life and that, in turn, can relieve the time pressures that most entrepreneurs and nonprofit executives experience. Our lives are far from nine-to-five, and any and all time-saving tips are worth considering.

For example, supermarket apps make it easy to keep track of what is on your shopping list—mine even lets me scan bar codes of the items I use—so that you don't find yourself making multiple trips to the store. A colleague uses the online shopping feature at her local market; the $15 shopping fee is well worth the time she saves by eliminating her weekly shopping trip, and the dollars she saves on impulse purchases. See if your local pharmacy has an app offering automated prescription refill features, and be sure to take advantage of your bank's automated and mobile capabilities.

Online calendars are a must for busy families. Find one that allows sharing with family members and be sure to take advantage of invitations and reminders so that spouses and children know when they have appointments or after school activities.

It is impossible to cover every app that is available these days; these are just a few that my colleagues and I have found to be particularly useful. New ones are being introduced all the time; who knows what wonderful tips and techniques will be available by the time you read this book?

Chapter Eight: Feeding and Maintaining Your Tribe

Every tip and trick in this book is intended to fire up your business by crafting and promoting your unique brand. If you have been implementing the suggestions in these chapters, you—as in your brand—look great! Your web presence, social media presence, and the in-person "you" presence tell the world that you are ready to take on customers and clients. In fact, by now you might even be a little overwhelmed by all the new people in your life!

So how do you keep it all going? How do you nurture all of these relationships so that they nurture you and your business in return?

Customer Relationship Management

This is where a customer relationship management (CRM) system comes in. There is such a wide variety of CRM tools that you should have no trouble finding the one that is right for you. I know some professionals who use Microsoft Outlook to manage their customer lists, others who use spreadsheets. Even though you are just starting out, you might want to begin with something a little more sophisticated—something that can grow with your business. These systems will keep you organized and help you manage a prospect from point of meeting right through the sale (or donation). **Salesforce** (www.salesforce.com) is very popular. The company offers a free trial period and modestly priced editions for small businesses, and special pricing for nonprofit organizations. **Contactually** (https://www.contactually.com) is mobile-friendly and also offers a free trial period.

Blackbaud® (www.blackbaud.com) is an industry leader when it comes to CRM systems for the nonprofit sector. Their Raisers Edge program is widely used in mid-sized to large organizations, but they also offer **eTapestry** for small and growing organizations. Again, free trials are available. **Bloomerang** (https://bloomerang.co) and **ELEO Online**® (http://www.eleoonline.com) are targeted to smaller nonprofits as well, and are billed as simple and completely cloud based.

Naturally, you will want to look at and compare pricing options when you choose a CRM. Here are a few other things to consider:

- How easy is the system to learn? To manage?

- How is technical support handled? Phone? E-chat? Email?

- How customizable is it? Weigh your desire for customization against the time you want to invest in learning and tinkering with your database.

- Can it help you to manage (i.e., store and find again) the information you want to capture about your clients or donors? How easy is this to do?

- Does the system offer cloud-based access, so that you can retrieve important client data while on the run? How well does it sync mobile and desktop entries, so that you can maintain your database, even while you are on the road?

- How can the system help you to analyze your data?

- Will the CRM system support an ongoing tickler system? It may seem like an easy thing to keep up with your tribe when you are just starting out, but this will change quickly as your database grows. So make sure that your CRM system supports the idea that you will need to be reminded to get in touch with people, so that you and your business remain in your ideal clients' consciousness.

I know I have mentioned **LinkedIn** a lot in this book, but I want to point out to you a few additional features that make LinkedIn a great "starter" CRM. First, the ability to sort by location is great for any time you travel. Going to a particular city? Sort your links to see which connections are living and working there. I also use the Relationship tab a lot. You can find it right under your under your contact's main header and photo. With it you can post a note, set a reminder (which will come to you via email), record how you met, and assign a tag. I tag my LinkedIn contacts by industry so that I can sort my list accordingly for announcements of upcoming events. Industry tags could also be useful for sharing ideas for future projects, or for highlighting recent successes. With all of this technology at your disposal, there is no need to rely on your memory!

Once you have the power to manage your contacts, you need a reason to contact them, right? Your every outreach can't be a selling point, either—remember the 80/20 rule? This is your opportunity to build a reputation as a resource, someone who is invested in their success as well as your own.

In Chapter Two I listed a number of newsfeed apps and you can always draw on these as a way to keep in touch. Keep your clients in mind as you read and tag (and send to them) articles that you think *they* might find useful. Here are a few other creative ways to show your appreciation of and support for your tribe:

- Send potential clients their way. Not every assignment you run across will be a good fit for you or your brand. Be open to arranging an introduction in person or via email or LinkedIn. Just be sure to follow up later to see how it all worked out. You also want to make sure your referrals reflect well on you!

- Congratulate them on a recent success. This is easier to do if you are already tracking them on Mention.net or Google Alerts. A phone call is unique these days, and note cards are still appreciated. Sendoutcards.com allows you to create a customized greeting card online that is then printed sent via snail mail.

- Thank them for whatever they might have done to help you. Again, phone calls, emails and personal notes are always appreciated. Include a photo if you are thanking someone for volunteering for an event or as a conference speaker.

- Ask for a referral or recommendation for your LinkedIn profile. If they post a recommendation on LinkedIn, ask permission to use it on your website too!

Always be thinking about how one client or customer can lead to another. It's pretty rare for anyone to stay in one job or location forever, so don't be shy about asking for referrals and be sure to keep in touch with those who are moving on to a new employer or city.

Don't be afraid of collaborations with fellow entrepreneurs. Your acquaintances in allied businesses can significantly expand your scope of products and services, and clients. For example, a freelance writer might partner with a website designer to elevate the scope and quality of each other's work. A photographer might team with a tour guide director to deliver professional-quality mementos of each tour experience. Take the time to outline roles, responsibilities and compensation ahead of time, so that everyone leaves the joint venture feeling as though they gained from the experience. Collaborations and referral systems can be especially valuable for nonprofit organizations. In fact, chambers of commerce often establish a community council to make it easier for local nonprofits to share calendars and refer clients. If your chamber doesn't have one, offer to launch it (remember my advice in Chapter Four about taking on a volunteer leadership role to "magnify your business or organization").

If you are in business for any length of time, it is likely that sooner or later you will run into a customer or client situation that doesn't go very well. It is best if you can head off trouble before it gets out of hand, by outlining clear service or product terms. If your business involves consulting, you might bring in a subcontractor whose expertise might be a little different than yours—but be clear with the client that you are considering this and be even clearer about who will be picking up the added cost. The point is, do what you can to rectify the situation, even if you know the relationship will end.

And if the relationship must end, be as gracious as you can be to avoid burning a bridge. Most of all, avoid taking the issue online in any way. If your customer or client takes it there, then think carefully before responding. My advice is to validate the customer's concern, pledge a desire to make things right, and take the conversation offline.

Final Thoughts...

As a small business owner or nonprofit executive, you've worked hard to build your brand. I thought it would be important to discuss protecting what you've built. Think about that sand castle you built at the beach as a child…..didn't you want to protect it from "the big wave"? Today, that big wave can come in many forms, so let's take a look at measures you can take to protect yourself.

Cybersecurity

It seems that hardly a week goes by that we don't hear about a major data breach in a large corporation. If they are vulnerable, you can bet that you are, too. I advise you to seek out a professional in your region who specializes in managed IT services. A call to your local Chamber should turn up at least one firm you can interview. Here are just a few things you need to be concerned with:

- Are your virus & malware definitions up to date? How often are you running a scan?

- Are you using secure cloud services? Many of the free versions may not be providing the level of security you need for your business.

- How are you backing up your data and how often?

- Do you allow employees remote access to your corporate data from laptops using free WiFi connections?

- What is your organization's plan if a laptop or smartphone goes missing or stolen?

- Does your company promote a BYOD (Bring Your Own Device) policy and what are your company's policies for such devices? Consider who is liable if a breach occurs.

- Do you conduct e-commerce or collect donations on your website via credit card processing? How are you handling PII (Personally Identifiable Information)? You should understand your state's laws around this in order to be compliant with reporting of breaches.

- If you are sending email with PII, are you using an email encryption service so that it can't be intercepted by hackers?

While this isn't an exhaustive list, it has hopefully started you thinking about the steps necessary to open a dialogue with a competent professional in your community.

Protecting Intellectual Property

Intellectual Property laws go beyond protecting inventions. They help protect your logos, business name, and ideas. Briefly, here are the various protections available to you, as explained by the Small Business Administration http://www.sba.gov:

- **Patent**: A patent for an invention is the grant of a property right to the inventor. Patents are granted for new, useful and non-obvious inventions for a period of 20 years from the filing date of a patent application, and provide the right to exclude others from exploiting the invention during that period. (Author's note: you may file for a provisional patent before deciding whether to fully pursue your application. Patent development costs can become prohibitive for smaller companies.)

- **Trademark**: A trademark is different than a patent since it only protects words, names, symbols, sounds, or colors that distinguish

- **Copyright**: The Library of Congress registers copyrights, which last for the life of the author plus 70 years. Books, movies and musical recordings are all examples of copyrighted works. (Author's note: you can't copyright an idea—merely the expression of an idea.)

Adding to the confusion, is protecting what you've created in a social media world. I suspect this will only be heightened in the years to come. One article on the SBA's website might be particularly interesting for you to peruse, entitled "5 Tips for Protecting Your Business Intellectual Property in a Social Media World". Here's the website for this article: https://www.sba.gov/blogs/5-tips-protecting-your-business-intellectual-property-social-media-world

If you suspect you have built anything worth protecting from an intellectual property point of view, you might want to consult with a local business attorney specializing in intellectual property protection for advice on how to proceed. Certainly,

(continued from previous: goods and services. Trademarks, unlike patents, can be renewed forever as long as they are being used in commerce.)

if you feel there have already been violations, legal action might need to be taken.

Insurance

Here's another instance for reaching out to your "tribe" to see who they would recommend locally as an insurance broker or agent specializing in helping you assess your risks and exposure. Generally, there are various types of insurance that your small business or nonprofit might need to have in place in order to protect not only the organization, but the employees (and volunteers) behind it. The main types of insurance include: General Liability Insurance; Product Liability Insurance; Professional Liability Insurance (also known as Errors and Omissions Insurance); Directors and Officers Insurance; Commercial Property Insurance; Home-Based Business Insurance; and Cyber Liability Insurance policies. Seek professional guidance to understand what will work best for you.

In conclusion, I hope this book has helped you launch your new initiative or it has given you ideas for taking it to the next level. Only when you "magnify your business or organization" will you know if you've got what it takes to succeed. Wishing you much success and prosperity in your endeavors!

Acknowledgements

This book would have never been published without the gentle prodding and encouragement from my own tribes, both professional and personal. Thank you to the members of my networking groups and associations, especially Val Waterman, Abby O'Neill, Carol Camerino, Michele Hickey, and Dennis C. Miller. You all knew this would be possible for me even before I could conceive the vision. A big thank you to Michele Hickey of Silver Lining Communications and Barry Cohen of AdLab Media Communications for their editorial help.

I am forever grateful to my family for giving me the opportunity to magnify my own business throughout the years. Bob, Sara & Kristen….. I love you all! And, my Mom…my biggest cheerleader yet. Thank you for always believing in me.

Maria Semple is the Founder and CEO of The Prospect Finder LLC. She is an experienced researcher, trainer, and frequent speaker on prospect research, email marketing and simple social media strategies. She consults with nonprofit organizations, financial services firms and small businesses interested in finding their best prospects for long-term business relationships. She is a regular monthly contributor to the Tony Martignetti Nonprofit Radio Show, available on iTunes. Maria Semple previously authored two downloadable and interactive e-books, "Panning for Gold", filled with dozens of prospecting resources.

Maria's firm is also a Master Certified Constant Contact Solution Provider, assisting small business owners and nonprofits with their email marketing needs and social media strategies. Maria is a Constant Contact Authorized Local Expert, enabling her to deliver seminars on leveraging the power of Email Marketing and Social Media. Finally, as a "LinkedIn Evangelist", Maria helps nonprofits and small businesses understand how to use this free tool to increase visibility.

Maria currently resides in New Jersey with her husband and two daughters. She actively volunteers with organizations in her local nonprofit community including the Women's Leadership Council of United Way of Northern New Jersey, Fairleigh Dickinson University, Financial Women's Association, and Financial Planning Association of New Jersey.

She dreams of a future surrounded by palm trees and sailing the Caribbean.

Visit her website at www.TheProspectFinder.com for free resources and additional information.

www.ingramcontent.com/pod-product-compliance
Lightning Source LLC
Chambersburg PA
CBHW030806180526
45163CB00003B/1159